STOLEN MUMMIES

STOLEN MUMMIES

Ain't Got No Press

Design, and Layout ~ Rick Lupert
Front and Back Cover Photos ~ Sarah Kobrinsky
About the Author Photos ~ Self-service PhotoCard Machine

Thanks to Sarah, Gideon, Brendan, Amélie, The Lyons Family, Havurah, Young Brits Willing To Curse on Tape, Queen Elizabeth The II, and French Girls Everywhere.

(818) 904-1021

or

15522 Stagg Street
Van Nuys, CA 91406

or

Rick@PoetrySuperHighway.com

or

http://PoetrySuperHighway.com/

First Create Space ~ June, 2008

Printed by CreateSpace.com
United States of America

ISBN: 978-0-9727555-2-8 $10.00

to Sarah and Gideon

introduction

A few days ago (Daylight Savings Time), a thirty five year old man residing in Hollywood California, a mythological city boasting more gods than voters, was a victim of a psychotic episode already referred to by the local deities as "The Recent Episode". For a space of about seventy two hours, or until the effects of a collection of poems entitled Stolen Mummies, by Rick Lupert, had worn off, the man believed himself to be the adventurous author of the same volume. His behavior during this period, while pleasant enough toward the landlord and other tenants of the building in which he lives, was marked by spells of random furniture moving and assertions (to no one in particular) that his apartment had been invaded by "Englishmen". Fortunately, his pet cat (Maggie), who had seen him through a previous seizure in which he insisted he was the late S.J. Perelman, was equipped to deal with these peculiarities. She amended his daily diet to include indigenous rodents and flying insects, added her name to the lease (albeit misspelled), and purchased several Thousand-Piece Jigsaw Puzzles (depicting a variety of domestic Norwegian scenes) to occupy him while his former identity reassembled.

Since then, the man has steadily returned to his former self and has even taken on several writing projects, including the introduction to the aforementioned Stolen Mummies. The following is an excerpt from that effort: "Rick Lupert is an honest poet. He has an honest face. His mouth is honest. His words are honest. The sentences he makes with those words (either spoken or written) are honest. Even the complete fabrications that emerge from the pages of his latest book positively sizzle with integrity. When, for instance, he describes his recent trip to England and the fascinating

encounters he has with the people of that proud country, you can almost believe that he went there. My Irish mother used to say (the others hardly spoke to me unless I pretended to be my sister) 'There is nothing crazy about thinking there are Englishmen hiding behind the sofa. The craziness is in looking for them'. Well folks, so keen are the subtleties of Mr. Lupert's poetry, the reader may wonder if closing the cover of this slender book is enough to keep the British Commonwealth described therein from running amuck in your home."

As one who may not have had the privilege of meeting the man who penned these lines before his "Recent Episode", you the reader may none the less surmise that his mind is on the mend and that his lucidity with the written word, for the most part, proves it. Now, do you think you could grab the other end of this couch and help me move it away from the wall? I just want to see how many people I have to shop for.

Brendan Constantine
June 12, 2002

"On thinking about Hell, I gather my brother Shelley found it was a place much like the city of London. I who live in Los Angeles and not in London find, on thinking about Hell, that it must be still more like Los Angeles."

Bertolt Brecht

"I have been assured by a very knowing American of my acquaintance in London, that a young healthy child well nursed is at a year old a most delicious, nourishing, and wholesome food, whether stewed, roasted, baked, or boiled, and I make no doubt that it will equally serve in a fricassee, or a ragout."

Jonathan Swift
A Modest Proposal

RESPIRATOR, n. An apparatus fitted over the nose and mouth of an inhabitant of London, whereby to filter the visible universe in its passage to the lungs.

Ambrose Bierce
The Devil's Dictionary

"I had been in London innumerable times, and yet till that day I had never noticed one of the worst things about London--the fact that it costs money even to sit down."

George Orwell
Down and Out in Paris and London

Let's Go London

I

Airplane wings
look like diving boards
except instead of swimming pools
you plummet to your death

II

On the way to London
I read through the dictionary
I should be fluent by the time we land

III

My Mother's Last Words of Advice:

Don't fuck Big Ben.

haiku

There are Africans
dancing outside the window
of my London home

Eric Clapton

I am sitting on a red bed in Hackney
Downstairs a Canadian types
Bonjo came by earlier to collect his mail

So did the television police
to collect the television tax
Sarah tells him they don't watch TV

He wants to see if it has an arial
She won't show him because
I'm still sleeping in that room

That's right
They put the American
in the room with the TV

Thought I'd be more comfortable
Figured Americans travel with their own arials

Figured the TV police
wouldn't have picked this week
to pop in

Sign in Gatwick Airport

Female toilets, straight ahead

The English society so open
they parade their fetishes
just this side of Passport Control

Swimming

Just downstream from the tower of London
is a small globe like building
It is the testicle of London

Message Written in Guestbook at the British Museum

Send the Greek Marbles back to Athens
30/7/2001

I write in "Bring the mummies back to life" and go to the museum cafe

Covent Garden August

The women of London
all in summer dresses
spaghetti strap strings
every one of them

It is amazing
it is wonderful
it is stupendous
It is orchards of still life

under cloud-free sky
It is hourglass curves
accentuated with
new millennia fashion

It is standing outside
The Covent Garden Tube Station
Giving Athena the forty P. she needs
for the ride home

A Covent Garden Statue

unusually animated on her cigarette break
blowing smoke into the air
instead of balloons

At The Tower of London

I

I want to use the Medieval Norman bathroom
        in White Tower
but the hole is covered with glass
So I head off to Bloody Tower
and go there

II

In the Crown Jewel Building
there is a solid gold coronation spoon
Undoubtedly used by Elizabeth to eat Wheaties
the day she became queen

Housing The Crown Jewels

I resist the urge to buy English Flag boxer shorts
I don't know the the queen would feel
about my willy touching her precious colors

Dinner

There is a convenience store in London
called Absolutely Starving
I'd imagine if you're that hungry,
you're not so worried about convenience

Coffee-fest Destiny

I'm glad there is a Starbucks here
It reminds me that all cultures are becoming the same
and soon I won't have to waste money
travelling anymore

Alone at the London Dungeon

on the south bank
A complete stranger
offers to chop off my head for the picture

British Hospitality

Dialogue for a Habitat

ring ring

    Hello?

London calling

    click.

In The Road

At Abbey Road
a cab driver killed me with his cab
as I posed at famous Beatles walk
I've lived a good life

Bock?

The Piccadily Tube line
terminates at Cockfosters

I've already said too much

Snoozing Comrade

A man on the Tube
falls asleep
holding an open copy of
something by Karl Marx

Perhaps if Marx
wrote more engaging prose
Communism wouldn't have failed

At Finchley Central

I saw a man so bald
he made Telly Savalas
look like Sasquatch

Voulez Vous?

After I met Yael from Lyons in Finchley Central
I started to translate everything I knew into French

Words like "need" and "most" and "I want you
to come live with me in Los Angeles forever"

to have handy for our second encounter
at the museum the next day

She speaks some English, but these things
are better done in her native tongue

Wednesday Night Dinner With Gideon's Family in Finchley

They buy him birthday cake
shaped like plumber's ass

Father tells stories
about the entire world

Mother pretends she baked the bread
so I'll eat it

Sister rings back the Indian restaurant
since they forget the birthday lamb

Family cat does the tango
across the kitchen floor

Meows
louder than Elvis

At the Tate Modern

I

Pardon me
have you seen two beautiful French girls

II

"Mon oeuvre est ma pretention"

Ben Vautier

III

Waiting for two French girls
in the lobby

still life with Rick

IV

at the untitled sculpture by Robert Gober

Two girls giggle at leg
coming out of wall

I'd like to make art
that makes two girls giggle

V

at *Memorial to the Sacred Wind* by Jean Tinguely

This machine
could be the death of me
Metal
I'm standing in the wrong place
waiting to view its operation
War machine. Rust.
Here she comes
I'm dead
I always die
at museums

VI

Sitting between two empty spaces
I slide over so a couple can sit together
I never have this problem

At The British War Museum

Six keys
on a key ring
excavated from Ponary Forest
Pits meant for petrol tanks
filled with Jewish bodies
Six doors
never unlocked

Secret Agent Man

Travelling alone without a watch
One becomes skilled at
spying on other people's wrists

Idle conversation in the Pub During the Jack the Ripper Tour

"It must suck to be stabbed to death by a maniac"

"Yeah"

A Period Piece

The Jack The Ripper tour guide
tells us that prostitutes of the time
performed the *Four Penny Knee Trembler*
She encouraged us to use our imagination
to determine what that was
You should do the same

It's A Dog's Life

A woman brushed oil onto hot dogs
in a cart outside Westminster Abbey

She's brushing the dogs of
ancient Christian martyrs

I wonder how Sir Thomas of Croix
feels about them selling lemonade

up against his tomb

Inside the Shore Exhibit
in the London Aquarium

There are signs that say "Come and touch me"
I should put some of those up in my apartment

At the Royal Academy of Arts Masterpieces of French Painting Exhibition

hangs *View of the Gare St. Lazare Paris,* 1887,
oil on canvas, by Norbert Goenutte
It was purchased in 1888 by one George Lucas
These days he only buys watercolor reliefs of C3P0

Picking Up Glass on the Piccadily

I

I am picking up glass on the Piccadilly
Not the circus
the road
There is glass on the sidewalk
Right by the road
I am picking it up
I'm no martyr
Didn't break it
Just picking it up
imagine
Little Prince William
Hopping barefoot up the road
blocks away from the palace
Cuts his royal feet
spills his royal blood
Plebian like me
slip on the blood
break open the head
Sue Royal Family
for a piece of England
Turmoil
Disaster
Must pick up glass

II

I want a car
I want a smart car
I want a car that is smart
Six feet long
steering wheel on left
where, it knows, I want, it to be
Smart car
Six feet long
Fits only me
Want to carry someone else?
Have to get another car
At these prices
can afford two
Smart car
It's smart
You're smart
Smack me
ooh, it smarts
Want to buy smart everything
Smart jam
smart teeth
smart man
do my taxes
do my taxes smart man
You so smart
look smart too
in your smart car
(I want)

III

Enter green park
green striped chairs everywhere
Think "How nice
Comfy chairs for everyone."
Sit in chair
write part one
man with machine comes
says
"One pound for the sit"
"I'm sorry?"
"One pound for the sit in the chair."
"I had no idea
I'll get up
I have no interest
in paying to sit down"
Get up
Everyone leaves
except the chair
walk to tree
sit on root of tree
tree free

IV

Go to palace
Wait?
one hour
Wait?
two hours
Wait?
six days
Wait?
Come back in your next life.
Buy ticket
Must see throne
Royal hiney sit there
Buy ticket
Wait
palace
throne

Jacket Famine

I order jacket potatoes
because it's chilly
but they don't come in my size
so I sit down
have a coffee
eat them

Not Tubular

You can take the Tube
anywhere in London
unlike in Los Angeles
where if you don't have a car
they shoot you in the head
because you're no good
to society

I Wanted to Stay Anyway

The girl working the cafe with the jacket potatoes
asks everyone if they want their food to take away
Except for me who she tells to have a seat
I think it's because she wants my American body
She's put aphrodisiac in the cheese

Friday Night With the Jews in Finchley

We light the same candles
say the same prayers
sing the same melodies (almost)
In this international city
we all speak the same language

At Buckingham Palace

I

The chair in the guard room
is worth more than everything
I've ever owned

II

Contrary to my observation in Versailles
This is the nicest single family residence
I have ever seen

III

Using the lavatory
at Buckingham Palace
I'll spare you the details

Manu Chao in the Morning

which is to say,
the afternoon

Sunday, after evening
of Nargilah viewing

tall beer cans
making the British swear

Somehow the blinds
don't conceal England's sun

as we eat morning cheese
fondle morning cat

pack for termination
at the sea

Havdallah Under Finchley Rain

twisted birthday candles
familiar melody
water comes from the sky
as we call for Eliyahu
filing inside
Maybe the messiah
will come next week
with umbrella
for eternal
dry
Sabbath

Fudge the cat

back legs don't work
tangos across kitchen floor
meows like plantation field spiritual
rubs against
anything that is

England is the Perfect Place to Shave My Head

Everyone offers to do it
Leah Kobrinsky says
"Bitch, It'll grow back"

La Manche

One Sunday we drive to the coast
I get out of the car

walk towards France
Paris

Tu es la plus belle femme
que j'ai jamais vu

Train to the Plane

Southwest bound train
British rail to Salisbury, Stonehenge

Tour-book says It's easy to get there
If you aren't carting forty five ton rocks

I sit in First Class Seat
because I don't know any better

sipping darjeeling with honey
bought from Cuppaccino boy

Who made like he wanted me
I only go for French girls

So I'm on the train alone
with airplane seats

fold down tables
no room for legs

While Britain goes by me
like sideways TV

Be Prepared

Walking through London
I find a half shequel coin in my pocket
You never know when
the Messiah's going to comes

Letter From Stonehenge

Dear Reader
I write to you from Stonehenge
Salisbury Plane
Where five thousand years ago
pre-historics moved stones
heavier than a lions ego
to this circle to tell the months
or chart the universe
or slaughter the living
never dreaming of
gift-shop
or even England

They don't let you touch the stones any more
modern humans chipping off souvenirs
like it's the Berlin Wall.

I have the Berlin Wall
re-assembled in horseshoe circle
in my back yard
put together from bits
I've chiseled off of historic sites
around the world

Every night I dress in secret clothes
and run from one side to the other
cheering
I'm free
I'm free
I'm five thousand years old
I'm English field full of oblivious sheep
I'm driving the A303 to London
I'm a spinach pie
I'm layers of clothing
I'm black woman with yellow jacket
I'm heavy rock
lying down
on holiday
married to history
I'm free
Twenty minutes to the next bus
Swords in the forest
Umbrella larger than life
Second floor transportation
I am Ringo
I am Charles
I am writing you from Stonehenge
Kiss all the babies
write back
see you soon

Let's Talk About the Weather

Summer in London
is like Winter in Los Angeles
Depending on whether it's Tuesday or Wednesday
and sometimes on whether
it's 11am or noon

Happy Pigs

in farm field
graze oblivious to sign above:

Pork, Sausage, Fresh

They Say That Water Ruins Leather

Does that mean that cows are no good
after the rain?

Revelation

The walking tour of Jack the Ripper's London
and the walking tour of Old Jewish East End
begin and end in the same spot
Leading me to the inevitable conclusion
that Jack the Ripper
was, in fact
Moses

Jerusalem

In New York City
and in London

Jews settled in the east
Whatever city we live in

We are always
thinking east

Rolling Blackout

Ten days
and my nineteenth anniversary
as a Californian

I am reminded of this
on the train to Gatwick
when the electricity goes out

and I'm left
writing in the dark
There are apologies

Eventual movement
to another train
platform thirteen

non-stop
gonna see the folks I dig
California, I'm coming home

PHOTOCARD

Name of Holder: Mr.Mrs.Miss.Ms.

Rick Lupert

Valid for use only by person
shown with a ticket bearing
the same number

BJI 7076

RSP 3588/9

about the author

Rick Lupert has been involved in the Los Angeles poetry community since 1990. He served for two years as a co-director of the Valley Contemporary Poets, a twenty-three year old nonprofit organization which produces a regular reading series and publications out of the San Fernando Valley. His poetry has appeared in numerous magazines and literary journals, including *The Los Angeles Times, Chiron Review, Zuzu's Petals, Caffeine Magazine, Blue Satellite* and others. He recently edited *A Poet's Haggadah: Passover through the Eyes of Poets* anthology and is the author of ten other books: *Paris: It's The Cheese, I Am My Own Orange County, Mowing Fargo, I'm a Jew. Are You?, I'd Like to Bake Your Goods, A Man With No Teeth Serves Us Breakfast* (Ain't Got No Press), *Lizard King of the Laundromat, Brendan Constantine is My Kind of Town* (Inevitable Press), *Feeding Holy Cats* and *Up Liberty's Skirt* (Cassowary Press). He has hosted the long running Cobalt Café reading series in Canoga Park since 1994 and is regularly featured at venues throughout Southern California.

Rick created and maintains the Poetry Super Highway, a major internet resource for poets. (PoetrySuperHighway.com)

Currently Rick works as the music teacher and graphic and web designer for Temple Ahavat Shalom in Northridge, CA and for anyone who would like to help pay his mortgage.

Rick's Other Books

A Man With No Teeth Serves Us Breakfast
Ain't Got No Press
May, 2007

I'd Like to Bake Your Goods
Ain't Got No Press
January, 2006

BRENDAN CONSTANTINE IS MY KIND OF TOWN
Inevitable Press
September, 2001

up liberty's skirt
Cassowary Press
March, 2001

FEEDING HOLY CATS
Cassowary Press
May, 2000

I'm a Jew, Are You?
Cassowary Press
May, 2000

MOWING FARGO
Sacred Beverage Press
December, 1998

Lizard King of the Laundromat
The Inevitable Press
February, 1998

I Am My Own Orange County
Ain't Got No Press
May, 1997

Paris: It's The Cheese
Ain't Got No Press
May, 1996

www.ingramcontent.com/pod-product-compliance
Lightning Source LLC
Chambersburg PA
CBHW060429050426

42449CB00009B/2199